THE STORY OF

# MUHAMMAD ALI,
## Heavyweight Champion
## of the World

BY BARRY DENENBERG

## A YEARLING BOOK

## ABOUT THIS BOOK

The events described in this book are true. They have been carefully re-searched and excerpted from authentic autobiographies, writings, and commentaries. No part of this biography has been fictionalized.

To learn more about Muhammad Ali, ask your librarian to recommend other fine books you might read.

*For Efrat Ginot*

Published by
Dell Publishing
a division of
Bantam Doubleday Dell Publishing Group, Inc.
666 Fifth Avenue
New York, New York 10103

ISBN: 0-440-40259-X

Published by arrangement with Parachute Press, Inc.
Printed in the United States of America
January 1990

10  9  8  7  6  5  4  3  2  1
OPM

# Contents

*I don't have to be what you want me to be.*
*I'm free to be who I want.*

*Muhammad Ali*

# Introduction

Cassius Marcellus Clay, Jr., later known to the world as Muhammad Ali, was one of the greatest heavyweight boxers of all time. Some say he was the best, ever. He dominated boxing from the time he won the 1960 Olympic gold medal when he was eighteen years old, until he retired from the ring twenty years later. He won the Heavyweight Championship of the World three times.

No athlete in history was as well-known as Muhammad Ali. When he fought, it was news; and when he didn't fight, it was news. That's because he was important for more than his boxing achievements. He is important because his life has been a mirror of the times in which he has lived. When we read his story, we begin to understand more about America during the

1

1960s and 1970s—a time of deep unrest in this country. And we begin to understand what it was like to grow up as a black person during this period of great change.

Muhammad Ali was at the center of the two most important issues of the times—the Vietnam War and the Civil Rights Movement. He will be remembered as a great boxer *and* a great fighter.

# The Kid From Louisville

Cassius Marcellus Clay, Jr. was born on January 17, 1942. His father, Cassius Clay, Sr., known as "Cash," was outgoing, talkative, and a very good dresser. He liked to sing and act; and when he stepped onto the dance floor, everyone stopped to watch. Some people said he was a loudmouth and a know-it-all.

Cash owned a sign-painting company that produced many of the signs on the trucks and buildings in Louisville, Kentucky, where the family lived. He was twenty-eight when he married seventeen-year-old Odessa Grady.

Cassius Jr.'s mother was old-fashioned. She didn't drink or smoke and made sure that Cassius went to the Baptist Church every Sunday. She was quiet and liked to keep to herself. Cassius Jr. was lucky enough to inherit her good looks.

When Cassius was born, his mother was sure she did not have the right baby in her bed. He was too quiet to be a Clay. Sure enough, she was right. The nurses rushed back to the nursery to bring her the right baby: a crying, little Cassius.

Just as soon as they got Cassius home from Louisville General Hospital, his parents began to spoil him. His mother was pleased with everything he did. His father never stopped talking about his son.

Cassius was only ten months old when he started talking. Everyone in the family swears his first words were "Gee Gee." Later, Cassius boasted that even as a baby he knew he wanted to become a champ. He said that "Gee-Gee" stood for Golden Gloves, a title he would win one day.

Cassius Jr.'s mother spent many hours playing with him. He did not like sitting still. He was so strong that one day he accidentally hit her in the mouth. One of her teeth was loosened so badly that it had to be removed. In later years Mrs. Clay bragged that this was her son's first punch. She claimed it showed he was a born fighter.

Cassius had a nickname for his mother. He called her "Bird" because she was as "pert and pretty" as a bird. After a while everyone started calling her that.

Cassius Sr. frequently went around the house saying that his son was "just as pretty as a picture." When Cassius Jr. was starting to try out his soon-to-be-famous legs, he ran right into the edge of the dining room table. Aside from almost taking out an eye, he managed to cut himself badly. "I hope we don't mess up that pretty face," his father said. Not long after that, Cassius Jr. was caught looking in the mirror saying, "I hope I don't mess up that pretty face."

The handsome boy was raised in an atmosphere of love and attention. Relatives were always visiting the Clay house now that there was a new baby. Cassius loved the activity, and he loved being spoiled by aunts, uncles, and grandparents. He spent a lot of time at his Aunt Coretta's house. It was the best place for his mother to leave him when she went to work. Aunt Coretta's house was also a small restaurant and a bakery. When he was there, Cassius tried to eat everything in sight. He especially liked her famous taffy.

Cassius's brother, Rudolph Valentino Clay, was born just thirteen months after Cassius. Rudy was a welcome addition to the family—especially as far as Cassius was concerned. The two brothers shared a room and did almost *everything* together. Cassius was a loving and protective older brother.

Mrs. Clay did the washing, cooking, and cleaning for a white family that lived in a better part of Louisville. She also helped take care of their children—all for four dollars a day. Nearly every morning she left for work before Cassius was up.

When Cassius was old enough to take care of himself and keep an eye on his brother, he would wait outside, watching for "Bird" to come home. Cassius often hoped she would bring hot dogs and hamburgers for dinner. Many times, though, she was too tired from working to cook anything at all.

Even when Cassius was little, he was aware that there were two different worlds in Louisville: the white world and the black world. One day he and his mother were downtown. Cassius said he was thirsty. In those days Louisville, along with many other places in the South, was segregated. That meant that black people could not stay in the hotels, they could go to only one movie theater, and they could not be served food or drinks in the stores. Mrs. Clay decided to try to get a drink for her son anyway. The clerk behind the lunch counter said no, and the store guard made them leave. Cassius cried all the way home.

The Clays did not have much money. Their clothes were secondhand, and they mended their shoes by putting cardboard inside them. The Clay's four-room house was on Grand Avenue in the West End section of Louisville. The house was in need of repair. The roof leaked, the walls needed patching, and each year the porch seemed to sag a little more until it began to look as though it were about ready to fall off.

But things were not all bad. The Clays were fortunate enough to have a car, although it was an old one. Once Mr. Clay bought Cassius a new suit to wear to church on Sundays. And sometimes Mrs. Clay would come home from the grocer with chicken and potatoes for a family feast!

When Cassius was twelve, his father gave him a brand new bicycle. It was bright red with spotless whitewall tires. There were lights on the back and a spotlight up front. Cassius just couldn't wait to show it off.

One day he went riding with his best friend, Johnny Willis. It started to rain, and they decided to head for the Home Show. The Home

Show was a big fair held every year in Louisville. They liked all the free popcorn, hot dogs, and candy they could get there. As soon as they arrived, they began eating as much as possible. At the end of the day they were almost the last to leave. That's when they discovered that Cassius's bicycle was missing. Johnny and Cassius ran around asking if anyone had seen it. No one had. Someone suggested they go to the nearby Columbia gym to see Joe Martin who ran the gym.

Joe Martin was a policeman when he wasn't taking care of the gym. He told Cassius to tell him what had happened, and Joe wrote it all down. It didn't sound as if he would be able to find the bicycle.

But Cassius wasn't thinking about his bike anymore. He was too excited by what he saw around him—the sights and smells of a real boxing gym. In one corner a boxer was hitting the speed bag. Over in another corner there were two boys who were not much older than Cassius. They were jumping rope. In the ring one young boxer was shadowboxing so fast his arms were almost a blur.

Joe Martin noticed Cassius's interest. He gave him an application for joining the gym. Boxing lessons were given from six to eight o'clock on

Monday through Friday nights, he told him. Cassius tucked the application into his back pocket and headed home.

Mr. Clay wasn't happy when he heard about Cassius's bicycle. He yelled at his son for being so careless. Cassius apologized. He *had* been careless.

Cassius had lost his bicycle, but he had found his future.

# Learning the Ropes

That weekend Cassius watched a TV show called "Tomorrow's Champions." On the show, he saw Joe Martin working in the corner of a ring with one of the local amateur fighters. He told his mother that he was thinking about learning to box. They talked it over with his father. Both parents warned Cassius that there was no money to spare for carfare. But Mr. Clay thought learning to box might not be a bad idea.

Joe Martin had been an amateur boxer before he became a policeman. He liked to spend as much time as possible coaching his young boxers. Cassius, a thin twelve-year-old, began training at Joe Martin's gym right away. When he first started out, Cassius was eager to learn. He made the mistake of fighting one of the older boys too soon. He quickly got a bloody nose, but he didn't stop. Even when he was being beaten, he never quit.

Soon Joe Martin decided that the skinny Cassius would be a good fighter for his Saturday TV show. Joe liked his never-give-up attitude. Cassius won his first fight on a split decision. Mr. Clay was proud that his son had won his first fight. He went all over Louisville telling everyone that Cassius was going to be the next Heavyweight Champion of the World.

After his first victory, Cassius started training even harder. He was eager to learn as much as he could, as fast as he could. Soon, however, he lost for the first time. But instead of feeling discouraged, he decided to find out where his opponent had been taught to fight so well.

It was a place called the Grace Community Center. The trainer there was a quiet man named Fred Stoner. The equipment wasn't as good as it was at Joe Martin's. But Cassius could see that the fighters there were learning better skills. They could box better. They were able to counterpunch faster. Their timing and rhythm were something to see. He decided to train at *both* places.

Somehow he managed his busy schedule. After school he went to his job at Nazareth College.

There he dusted, swept the stairs, and cleaned the floors. He earned enough money to pay for his carfare to the gym. His next stop was Joe Martin's, where he trained from six to eight o'clock. Then he was off to Fred Stoner's gym, where he would train from eight until midnight.

Cassius trained hard. He usually started with one hundred left jabs. Then he jabbed and moved forward, and jabbed and moved back. Next, he did combinations—jab and hook, jab and hook—over and over. He practiced blocking punches and ducking them. His training usually ended with one hundred push-ups and one hundred deep knee-bends.

As the days zipped by, he learned more. He learned how to keep moving; how to move backward at just the right time; and how to avoid punches, leaning away from them at the last second. Cassius practiced so much that soon he could tell when a punch was coming almost *before* it was thrown. He would keep his head in range, hoping his opponent would try to hit him. Then, at just the right moment, he would lean back, just a fraction of an inch out of the way. He would step to the right or step to the left and throw a lightning-fast jab. Then he would begin moving all over again.

Each day, Cassius woke up at dawn to run. He skipped rope, making it fancier and harder all the time. The more he skipped rope, the better his footwork became. He shadowboxed every day, too. That helped his hand speed and his mental quickness.

Cassius started to specialize in defense. He began to develop his own way of retreating. He concentrated on the timing of his punches and when to pull back. He practiced every move until he had it memorized, and he didn't have to think. If he had to think while he was fighting, he knew the punch would take too long.

One day Cassius was coming home from the gym. He was fourteen, and he had been training for two years. He heard the roar of a crowd coming from a radio in a nearby parked car. He poked his head in the car window. The people inside were listening to a fight. When it was over, the winner was announced, ". . . Heavyweight Champion of the World, Rocky Marciano." Cassius loved the way that sounded.

From that moment on, he wanted to become the Heavyweight Champion of the World. It was all Cassius thought about. He told his parents, and he told his friends. He told anyone who would listen. He had no doubts about it. He told Joe Martin, but Joe *did* doubt Cassius's words. His doubt had nothing to do with Cassius's ability, but with his weight. At only 115 pounds, he didn't look like a heavyweight boxer. Joe suggested that Cassius give some thought to becoming the Lightweight Champion of the World. But that didn't have the same ring to it.

As often as he could, Cassius watched fights on TV, studying each boxer's moves. And as he watched, he thought to himself that he could beat them. Cassius didn't keep this opinion to himself. He bragged to anyone who would listen that some day he would be the Heavyweight Champ. The other boys at Joe Martin's gym grew tired of Cassius's boasting and began to dislike him. It became so bad that Joe had to threaten to ban him from the gym.

In 1958, when he was sixteen years old, Cassius won the Louisville Golden Gloves light-heavyweight crown. He went on to fight in the Tournament of Champions in Chicago. The tournament was in a huge stadium. It was the biggest stadium Cassius had ever seen.

There were three matches going on at the same time, and the crowd was yelling and screaming. Boys from all over the country participated. Cassius lost. It was the first amateur fight he had lost, but it just made him work harder.

By the time he was sixteen, Cassius had grown quite a bit. He was now almost six feet tall and weighed 170 pounds. For the past four years he had done almost nothing but train. He went to school and he worked, but he spent all his free time training.

His parents were pleased with what Cassius was doing. They were glad he was not hanging out on street corners like many boys his age. Mr. Clay went to almost every fight. Mrs. Clay preferred to stay at home, but she was just as proud of her son.

Cassius became one of the best-known boxers in Kentucky. He was even becoming known in the neighboring states where he traveled for fights and tournaments. In 1959 he won the national AAU (Amateur Athletic Union) light-heavyweight title. And his bragging hadn't stopped. He took to walking around the boxing ring, with his arms raised, saying he was the "prettiest and the greatest." He even started making up poems, predicting the round in which he'd knock out his opponent:

"This guy must be done
I'll stop him in one.

Cassius's boldness in predicting his fights made many people come to see him in the hope that he would lose. They almost always left disappointed.

During this time hardly a day went by when there wasn't some news about blacks in the South fighting for equal rights. Battles over equality between blacks and whites in cities throughout the South made newspaper headlines across the nation. In 1955 a fourteen-year-old black boy named Emmett Till was beaten to death in Mississippi for whistling at a white woman. Two white men were accused of the crime but were never punished. Cassius never forgot what happened to Emmett Till.

That same year a black woman, Rosa Parks, refused to move to the back of a bus in Montgomery, Alabama, just because the seats in the front of the bus were "For Whites Only." Her refusal led to a boycott of city buses in Montgomery led by a young reverend named Martin Luther King, Jr. He taught his supporters that peaceful protest was their only weapon.

Blacks in Montgomery refused to ride the

buses for more than one year. They organized car pools or walked to work. For many people the boycott meant hardships and sometimes even violence. But when it was over, buses in Montgomery, Alabama, were integrated. Blacks could sit where they wanted to.

This event marked the beginning of the Civil Rights Movement. At this time Cassius was a teenager. Travelling to various cities around the country to fight his matches exposed Cassius to the world outside of his hometown. In one city he bought a copy of *Muhammad Speaks*, a newspaper published by the Nation of Islam, a black religious organization whose followers were known as Black Muslims.

The articles that Cassius read in *Muhammad Speaks* were concerned with black pride. One article explained that when blacks were taken from their homes in Africa and sold as slaves in America, the slave owners gave them different names to replace their real African names. The names most American blacks went by were not their real names. *Muhammad Speaks* said that blacks had lost their identity when they lost their names.

Cassius became interested in what the Black Muslims were saying. Whenever he went to a city for a fight, he tried to find out if there was a Muslim temple there. If there was, he went and listened to the minister speak.

In 1960, when he was eighteen years old, Cassius won the AAU title again. This victory qualified Cassius for the Olympic trials to be held in San Francisco, California. The games themselves would be held in Rome, Italy, that summer.

Cassius had not been thinking about the Rome Olympics. He was thinking about turning professional right away. But Joe Martin was against it. He was older and wiser than Cassius, and he knew that Cassius should work his way to the top gradually.

When Cassius arrived in Rome, many fight fans already knew who he was. Those who didn't soon found out. His winning smile won him lots of friends. And although he was considered to be a showoff, he was polite to everyone.

Cassius enjoyed being on his own for the first time. He shook hands with people everywhere he went and told them he was going to win the Olympic gold medal. Soon he was one of the most popular athletes in the Olympic Village.

Cassius won his first two fights. The attendance at the final bout was bigger than expected because everyone had come to see Cassius. He won this one, too, earning the gold medal in the light-heavyweight division. It was his forty-fourth consecutive win. He was now an Olympic hero! Cassius reminded everyone that he had told them so. "I am the greatest," he proclaimed.

When Cassius stepped off the plane in Louisville, he was looking forward to a hero's welcome. His mother, father, and brother ran to meet him. Cassius had been gone for twenty-one days, the most time he had ever spent away from home.

There was a police escort from the airport to downtown. The people of Louisville, black and white, lined the streets trying to get a glimpse of their Olympic hero. A *Welcome Home Cassius Clay* sign was hung in front of his high school, and the mayor gave a speech. He said that Cassius's gold medal was his key to the city. "He's our boy, Cassius, our next World Champion," said the mayor. "Anything you want in town is yours."

Cassius found out, however, that "anything" did not even include a hamburger and a milk shake.

One hot summer's day he and his friend Ronnie King were out riding their motorbikes. Cassius was hungry, and he wanted to stop at a restaurant to get something to eat. Ronnie didn't think it was such a good idea, but Cassius insisted.

There was a white motorcycle gang inside. They wore black leather jackets with Nazi symbols and Confederate flags on the back. Ronnie and Cassius sat at the counter. They ordered hamburgers and milk shakes and were told that they would not be served.

Cassius was shocked. Was it possible, after his triumphant homecoming, that the waitress did not know who he was? Patiently, he said, "I'm Cassius Clay. The Olympic champion." Just to make sure she understood, Ronnie made Cassius pull the medal out from under his shirt. The answer remained the same: "We don't serve no niggers."

Cassius felt worse than he had ever felt in his life—embarrassment mixed with shock. He stared straight ahead, not moving. He thought of the mayor's speech about how his Olympic gold medal was his key to the city.

The motorcycle gang was laughing at Cassius, making fun of Louisville's Olympic hero. Ronnie wanted to fight, but Cassius did not. His professional boxing career was just beginning. A broken hand could end it before his first fight. He convinced Ronnie just to walk out to the parking lot with him. But the gang would not leave them alone. They wanted Cassius to give them his medal.

No matter what they did, Cassius and Ronnie could not avoid confrontation with the bikers. Fortunately, they escaped with only some cuts and bruises.

The two boys washed themselves off in a nearby river. Ronnie washed Cassius's medal. The red, white, and blue ribbon had become stained with blood. Cassius stared at his medal. It looked cheap, not like the glowing key to the future he once thought it was. In an instant he decided what he would do.

He walked onto the bridge that stretched across the river and headed for the middle of it. He stopped over the deepest part of the river and threw the medal into the water. Ronnie was astonished, but Cassius calmly watched it sink to the bottom and out of sight. Ronnie didn't understand. He thought Cassius had lost his mind. Cassius told him not to be upset. "The medal was a phony," he said to Ronnie. "We don't need it."

# The Contender

Now it was time for Cassius to consider his professional career. Offers were coming in from people everywhere who wanted to be his manager. World Champion Floyd Patterson's manager was interested. Archie Moore, the Light-Heavyweight Champion was, too, even though he still held the championship title and fought in matches himself from time to time. Even Rocky Marciano, who had retired undefeated from the ring, offered to become Cassius's manager. This was the same Rocky Marciano who had been declared Heavyweight Champion of the World on the car radio that day when Cassius was fourteen. There was a lot to think about.

Bill Faversham, a Louisville businessman, was interested in the young Olympic champion, too.

He organized ten Louisville millionaires who wanted to invest in Cassius. They called themselves the Louisville Sponsoring Group. They offered Cassius a $10,000 advance and $200 a month, saying they would also pay all of his expenses. In return, they would get half of Cassius's earnings.

Cassius and his parents met with Bill Faversham and accepted his offer. Cassius was not the first athlete run by a group of people, or a corporation. The Clay family celebrated. Cassius gave the $10,000 advance to his parents. Finally that sagging front porch was fixed, and they put a new roof on the house.

Cassius had his first professional bout on October 29, 1960, in Louisville's Freedom Hall. Over 6,000 fans turned out to see their Olympic hero. His opponent was Tunney Hunsaker, a tough fighter. Cassius was tired of fighting amateurs and was eager to test his skill against a real professional. All his years of hard work and training paid off. He won a unanimous decision.

But Cassius still had a lot to learn. He would need expert training if he was to be properly prepared for the work of professional boxing. Cassius's backers, the Louisville Sponsoring Group, decided to send him to Archie Moore's training camp. Archie was one of the most experienced fighters in the business. Cassius's backers hoped the older boxer would pass his wisdom and experience on to their young fighter.

Moore ran a training camp in the hill country outside of San Diego, California. The camp was known as the "salt mine" and the gym was called the "bucket of blood." A bucket outside the building was painted to look as if blood was spilling over the rim, and *Bucket of Blood* was painted on it in bright red letters.

The boxers were taught discipline and self-reliance. They chopped their own wood, prepared their own meals, and did all the chores. When they weren't doing this, they were running up and down the wooded hills surrounding the camp.

When Cassius set off for San Diego, his Louisville backers were sure that they had made the right decision. They were wrong. Right from the start Cassius didn't like Archie—and he didn't like the training camp, either. After just a few weeks, Cassius left the "salt mine" and returned home.

Cassius then contacted a boxing trainer named Angelo Dundee, whom he had met three years earlier, in 1957. Cassius, with his brother Rudy tagging along, had called on Angelo when he was in Louisville with one of his fighters. Cassius thought it would be a good idea for Angelo to meet him now, since someday, he announced, he was going to be the World Heavyweight Champion.

Angelo Dundee thought the skinny fifteen-year-old was a nice kid, in spite of his bragging ways. A year later Angelo was in Louisville again. This time Cassius caught up with him at the gym. Cassius wanted a chance to spar with Willie Pastrano, the boxer Angelo was training. Watching Cassius was "three minutes of pure pleasure," Angelo later said. Everyone stopped to watch Cassius's dazzling footwork. They were equally impressed with his speed and style.

Bill Faversham contacted Angelo Dundee to see if he would like to become Cassius's trainer. He offered Angelo a choice. Faversham would pay him either $125 a week or 10 percent of Cassius's earnings. Angelo didn't know how much money Cassius would make, so he took the $125.

Cassius's relationship with Angelo Dundee was the most important step in his blossoming professional career. He and Angelo were a perfect match right from the beginning. Angelo was a good listener, and Cassius was a good talker. Not only that, Angelo was a family man with six

25

kids of his own. He understood the young Cassius. He realized that he couldn't change his unique style of fighting.

Cassius broke almost every boxing rule. He did not punch to the body, and he held his hands at his sides, too low to protect his face. Odd as it might have looked to the experts, this style worked for Cassius. Instead of changing it, Angelo worked on improving the young fighter's skills and getting rid of any bad habits. He didn't tell Cassius what to do; instead he offered suggestions. He gave Cassius time to think his ideas over. And in the end, the two usually agreed.

Angelo improved Cassius's technique. Soon he was shooting his left jab with more authority, slipping away from punches more easily, and learning to punch with power.

Cassius already had his mind set on beating Floyd Patterson's record. At twenty-one years and ten months old, Floyd was the youngest man ever to win the Heavyweight Championship. Eighteen-year-old Cassius had only three years to reach his goal.

He spent most of 1960 working with Angelo in Miami, Florida. Besides his first professional fight, Cassius had only one other fight that year. He won it with a knockout in the fourth round.

In 1961 Cassius fought eight times and won

every fight—six of them by knockouts. But the most important thing that happened that year had to do with wrestling, not boxing.

In June Cassius was in Las Vegas, where he happened to see a wrestler named George Raymond Wagner. Wagner was well known to wrestling fans as "Gorgeous George." Gorgeous George was one of the first wrestlers to turn the sport into a big show. He wore fancy capes and had long golden hair. Before every bout he had the ring area sprayed with his personal perfume. He was known from coast to coast; and whenever he wrestled, he drew big crowds.

Gorgeous George made quite an impression on Cassius, and Cassius decided to play to the crowds from the ring just as the wrestler did. Wherever he went, Cassius told people that he was "the fastest, the prettiest, and the greatest."

Cassius's bold style came at a time when the world of boxing had become boring. The current Heavyweight Champion, Floyd Patterson, was shy and quiet. When Cassius appeared on the scene, some called him a bag of wind. But to others he was a breath of fresh air.

Cassius made bold predictions about the outcome of each fight. In October 1961 he was about to fight Alex Miteff. Before the fight he told everyone which combination of punches would knock Miteff out. And in the sixth round Cassius knocked Miteff out by the very combination of punches that he had predicted!

Experts now rated Cassius the number eleven contender for the heavyweight title. Cassius rated himself number two. After just two years and ten fights, at nineteen years of age, that was a pretty good record. Fight fans talked about how brash he was. And people who had never given boxing a thought seemed to know his name.

Cassius grew bolder with every bout. Before his fight with Willie Besmanoff, he said he was "embarrassed to get into the ring with this unrated duck." He knocked out the "duck" in the seventh round.

"I'm the greatest. I'm not supposed to be on the floor—Banks in four!" This is what he chanted to his audience in February 1962, before his bout with Sonny Banks. But Banks shocked Cassius, sending *him* to the floor for the first time in his professional career. At the count of two, though, Cassius was already up, and in the fourth round he won on a technical knockout.

Archie Moore, the former Light-Heavyweight Champion, who at one time wanted to be Cassius's manager, was now fighting as a heavyweight. By 1962 Archie Moore had been fighting for twenty-six years. He had over one hundred knockouts in his career. In his prime he had been one of the greatest fighters. Now he was flabby and out of shape. Some experts say he should not have been fighting at all. He was at least forty-three and maybe as old as forty-nine.

Just the previous year Cassius had acted in a movie called *Requiem for a Heavyweight*. He played a young boxer fighting an aging boxer. Now, fighting Archie Moore, he would be doing the same thing in real life.

Weeks before the fight both fighters came out with their lips flapping. Cassius predicted he would beat "Moore in four."

His footwork and the speed of his combinations would be too much for Archie, Cassius announced. He even had a new punch just for this fight. Cassius called it the "Pension Punch" and said it would retire Archie and put him on a pension.

Archie also had a new punch for this fight. It was called the "Lip Buttoner." Archie promised it would button the famous "Louisville Lip," one of the many nicknames Cassius had been given.

On November 15, 1962, the talking was over and the fighting began. The bout was shown on closed-circuit TV in theaters around the country. Seats in the Los Angeles Sports Arena were sold out, setting an indoor attendance record for California.

Cassius was too much for the aging Archie. He knocked Archie down three times in the fourth round and the fight was over. Cassius was now twenty years old and considered by most experts to be the fourth-ranked contender for the heavyweight crown.

In March 1963, Cassius went to New York City to fight Doug Jones. Jones was a top-ranked contender and had never been knocked out. Madison Square Garden was sold out. Cassius predicted,

"Jones like to mix
So he'll go in six.
If he talks jive,
I'll have to cut it to five.
And if he talks some more,
I'll cut it to four."

But Jones didn't fall in four—or five, six, seven, eight, nine, or ten. He gave Cassius more trouble than he expected. The fans started booing and throwing things. Now, however, all those long hours of training were paying off.

The fight was close, but Cassius finally won a split decision.

Now Cassius began to really think big. He wanted a chance to win the Heavyweight Champion of the World title. He wanted to fight Sonny Liston.

# "Float Like a Butterfly, Sting Like a Bee"

Charles "Sonny" Liston was a large, mean-looking man with a powerful punch. He was an ex-convict who had been taught boxing by the prison chaplain. In eleven years he had won thirty-five of his last thirty-six bouts.

On September 25, 1962, Liston fought Floyd Patterson for the Heavyweight Championship of the world. After only two minutes and six seconds, Liston knocked Patterson out. It was the first time a world heavyweight title-holder had been knocked out in the first round.

On July 22, 1963, they had a rematch. This fight lasted only four seconds longer than the first. People were already calling Liston one of the great heavyweight champions of all time. He was considered unbeatable.

Late in 1963 Liston agreed to fight Cassius.

Almost every expert said it was a mismatch. Few gave Cassius a chance, even though he was younger, fitter, and faster.

The odds were seven to one against Cassius, and people argued about how long it would take Liston to knock him out. There *was* one expert who thought Cassius had a chance, Joe Martin, Cassius's first trainer. "I don't believe Liston could ever beat Clay. Clay can run faster backwards than Liston can forward," he said.

Cassius had fought and talked his way into a shot at the championship. Now he decided to stir things up to make sure everyone wanted to see the fight. He hired a bus and decorated it with big posters: *Sonny Liston Will Go in Eight. The World's Most Colorful Fighter.* He drove the bus to Denver, Colorado, and parked it outside Liston's home. It was one o'clock in the morning. The police had to be called to make Cassius leave.

The weigh-in at the Miami Beach Convention Hall was tense. Liston had heard just about enough from "Gaseous Cassius." Cassius wore a shirt with *Bear Huntin'* embroidered in red on the back. He chanted, "Float like a butterfly, sting like a bee," over and over.

"I'm ready to rumble. I'll eat you alive," he screamed. Liston just sat there and stared. Cassius gestured and ran around the room. At one point he had to be restrained by his own people. His blood pressure rose so high, the fight was nearly called off. Finally, he was fined $2,500 for unsportsmanlike conduct. *Hysterical Outburst at Weigh-in, Clay Scared*, read the newspaper headlines that day.

Why was Cassius acting this way? Many people thought he was scared, or nervous. Some people thought he was just plain crazy. But Cassius later said, "I wanted Liston to know I was crazy. Only a fool isn't afraid of a crazy man. You'll see tonight."

Cassius entered the ring wearing a short white robe that said *The Lip* on the back. When the bell rang for the first round, he came out dancing, hands dangling at his sides. Daring Liston to hit him, he leaned back, moving and throwing jabs at the older fighter. Dance, dance, jab. Dance, dance, jab. Liston stalked Cassius, waiting to hit him with one of his powerful punches—he figured one was all it would take. But Cassius continued to circle, never giving him an easy target.

When the bell rang to end round two, they kept fighting for almost ten seconds before they could be separated. In the third round Liston's left eye started to look bad. Cassius's constant movement and lightning-fast combinations were frustrating the slow-moving Liston. Cassius was getting stronger while Liston was tiring.

When round four ended, Cassius's eyes were stinging. He couldn't see. He wanted Angelo to cut his gloves off so he could fix his eyes. Some of the medicine used between rounds to treat Liston's badly bruised left eye had gotten on Cassius's glove, Angelo later figured out. When Cassius rubbed his own eyes, the medicine came off and stung so badly he could hardly see.

When the bell rang for the fifth round, the referee shouted for Cassius to come out of his corner. Angelo popped in his mouthpiece and pushed him out to the center of the ring. "Run, run, run," were Angelo's instructions. Cassius kept shaking his head, hoping to clear his vision. It was a miracle that he made it through the round.

By the sixth round he could see again. He fought hard and well while Liston was running out of steam. When the bell rang for the seventh round, Liston didn't even get off his stool. There was something wrong with his shoulder. Cassius celebrated while Sonny Liston had his shoulder taped up.

Cassius Clay was now the Heavyweight Champion of the World!

# Muhammad Ali

When Cassius met with reporters in the days and weeks after the fight, he sounded like a different person. And, in a way, he was.

The change was not only in the way he spoke, which was in a calmer and softer manner. It was also in the way he thought. For quite a while he had been thinking about what it meant to be black in a world led by whites. On the outside he was still the bold showman—predicting his fights and bragging in rhyme. But inside he had become a serious young man—a serious young black man.

Even before the Liston fight there were rumors that Cassius had joined the Black Muslims. In fact he had, but he didn't want to say anything publicly until the time was right. He knew that many people, black and white, would not like what he had to say. Now that he'd won the heavy-weight championship, he believed he could tell the truth.

Cassius explained to the public that he had joined the Black Muslims because he agreed with what they stood for. The Black Muslims believed that white people had made them slaves, and that this caused black people to feel inferior to whites. Black Muslims believed in the separation of the races, not in integration. Integration, they said, would never change the feeling of white people that they were superior. Only a separate, independent black society could give blacks back their identity.

The Black Muslims were a controversial group. They did not vote in elections because they didn't recognize the government of the United States as their real government. They also did not serve in the armed forces because their god, Allah, disapproved of war.

In 1964 most black Americans were not interested in the message of the Black Muslims and the Nation of Islam. They wanted integration, not segregation. They didn't want a separate black society; they wanted equal rights in the society they were living in.

By the early 1960s, the Civil Rights Movement

was blossoming into a nationwide struggle with Martin Luther King, Jr. as its leader. Some of their goals were equal education, equal opportunity, and equal protection under the law.

In 1964, when Cassius Clay was the Heavyweight Champion of the World, Muslim beliefs were considered radical and extreme. Martin Luther King did not like what the Black Muslims stood for. He said that Cassius was in favor of exactly what black Americans were fighting *against*. Joe Louis, the popular black former Heavyweight Champion, agreed. He said that the things Cassius believed were the "opposite of what we believe in." The president of the World Boxing Association said Cassius was a "detriment to the boxing world."

Even his family was shaken. Cassius's brother Rudy had also become a Black Muslim, and Mrs. Clay was upset with the decision her sons had made. When news reporters asked Mr. Clay if Cassius Jr. was going to change his name, according to the custom of Black Muslims, Mr. Clay said he was not.

But not everyone was against Cassius. Angelo Dundee felt that Cassius had a right to choose his own religion. Howard Cosell, a popular sportscaster, said it was no one's business what religion Cassius wanted to practice.

Cassius *did* announce that he was changing his name. Clay was not his name, he explained. His grandparents had been slaves, and Clay was most likely the name of a slave owner, not a slave. He was going to change his name to Cassius X. The X would stand for the family name that had been lost.

A month later he announced that he was changing his name again. His name would now be Muhammad Ali, which meant "one who is worthy of praise." He spoke with confidence to reporters: "I know where I'm going, and I know the truth, and I don't have to be what you want me to be. I'm free to be who I want.

"Now I am king; I will choose the people who will surround me," Ali said. From then on, the most important person in his life became Herbert Muhammad, the son of Elijah Muhammad, the leader of the Black Muslims, or the Nation of Islam.

In 1966, when Ali's contract with the Louisville Sponsoring Group ended, Herbert Muhammad officially became Muhammad Ali's manager. Ali's relationship with his Louisville backers had been a good one. But it was still a case of white people managing black people. Ali wanted to change that, and now he could.

Ali trusted Herbert Muhammad completely.

And, fortunately, Herbert Muhammad and Angelo Dundee got along well. As important as Herbert Muhammad might be outside the ring, Angelo was the genius inside the ring.

Herbert and Ali became good friends. He instructed Ali in the teachings of his father. Herbert was warm and friendly, and when it came to business, he was serious and smart. In the future Ali would not make a decision without him.

# A Different Kind of Champion

After all the commotion surrounding Muhammad Ali's decision to become a Black Muslim and change his name, it was time for him to box again. Muhammad Ali's rematch with Sonny Liston was scheduled for November 2, 1964, in Boston.

Ali returned to the world of boxing just as he had left it. He appeared at press conferences wearing his *Bear Huntin'* jacket, only this time he added a spiked bear collar and a pot of honey. Things were almost as chaotic before this fight as they had been before the first fight. Ali chanted,

"If you like to lose your money
Be a fool and bet on Sonny."

Liston was expected to win this fight. Most people felt that Ali had won the first fight by accident. But that didn't shake Ali's confidence.

41

"Liston," he said, "is too ugly to be the champion."

But three days before the fight Ali suffered severe pains while he was eating dinner. He was rushed to the hospital, where doctors found he had a hernia. The fight was delayed until May 25, 1965.

Then another problem came up. The Massachusetts Boxing Authority decided that the promoters of the fight did not meet with their approval. They suspected that Liston and his backers might be involved with criminals. Boston had a great name as a city that supported honest sports, and the authorities did not want to allow any event that might involve dishonest people.

It looked as if the fight would never take place. Finally, the Maine Athletic Commission offered the use of a hockey arena in the small town of Lewiston. It was the smallest town chosen to stage a championship fight in forty years.

It was also the first time Ali would fight as a married man. He had surprised his friends when he married Sonji Roi in the summer of 1964. He had fallen in love for the first time.

Unfortunately, the marriage lasted only a short time. Sonji found it difficult to live with the rules Black Muslims set for how women were to behave and dress. She used makeup, which was forbidden by the Muslims. And she liked fashionable dresses, which also caused a problem. Muslim women were supposed to wear dresses that reached to the floor. Sonji Roi and Muhammad Ali were divorced in 1966.

Ali's recent marriage did not distract him from his work as a boxer. He trained hard for his fight with Sonny Liston, and his training paid off. The fight was over almost before it began.

At the bell, Ali came out and threw a quick right at Liston. He danced away and then hit Liston with a perfectly timed right cross to the chin. Liston went down so fast the crowd suspected that the fight was "fixed." Some were angry just because it was so brief. Fans at ringside who saw the punch said it "couldn't have crushed a grape." Others said Liston was knocked out because he never saw it coming.

There is a theory that says it is not the power of the punch that knocks a person out but the mental shock. According to this theory, a knockout occurs when the mind does not have time to warn the body. Some people say this is what happened to Sonny Liston.

Shouts of "Fix!" filled the arena as people jumped up from their seats. The referee made

Ali go to a corner of the ring. Ali had been standing over Liston gesturing for him to get up. He was screaming, "Get up, you bum. Get up and fight, you bum."

A ringside official told the referee that the fight was over. The count had already reached ten before Liston got up. According to some, the count went as high as twenty-four. The whole fight had lasted only one minute and fifty-two seconds.

Muhammad Ali had successfully defended his title for the first time. Now there were other fighters waiting for their chance to challenge him. Floyd Patterson was one of them.

Ali and Floyd Patterson met on November 22, 1965. Patterson called his challenge to Ali a "moral crusade." He said he would never call Ali by his new name. He would always call him Cassius Clay "because that's the way he was born." Ali, he said, was a disgrace to blacks and to whites because he believed in the separation of the races and violence. Floyd Patterson represented the feelings of many people in America who wanted to see Ali lose.

At twenty-three years old, Ali was taller, younger, bigger, and faster than Floyd Patterson. He also had an eight-inch reach advantage. Ali destroyed Patterson. The fight was considered one of the most one-sided in boxing history. It was also the cruelest.

Ali could have knocked Patterson out at any time, but he didn't. He hit him enough to hurt him but not enough to end the fight. In the tenth round a doctor was called in to look at Patterson. In the eleventh, Angelo Dundee screamed for Ali to knock him out and finish the fight. Finally, the fight was stopped in the twelfth round.

After the fight Ali said that his brutal treatment of Floyd Patterson was a lesson. He said he was sending a message that people had better get used to seeing him the way he was: "Black, confident, cocky; my name not yours; my religion not yours."

In the next twelve months Ali fought five times, winning each time. Four of the five wins were knockouts. On February 6, 1967, he fought Ernie Terrell, and the fight was even more brutal than the Patterson fight. Terrell, like Patterson, refused to call Ali by his new name. The attendance figures set an indoor record, and the fight was televised around the world by satellite.

The fight lasted all fifteen rounds. When the bell sounded at the end of the fifteenth, one of the most savage fights in boxing history was over. One of Terrell's eyes was swollen closed and the other was getting there. Terrell didn't even have the strength to cover his face with his hands. People at ringside were screaming for the referee to stop the fight. Ali looked as if he hadn't even been in a fight.

A month later Ali knocked out Zora Folley in the seventh round. Ali was now twenty-five years old. He had defended his title nine times and was still the undefeated Heavyweight Champion of the World. But he was about to take on the one opponent he couldn't beat.

# Ali vs. the Army

Muhammad Ali had registered for military service, as required by law, shortly after his eighteenth birthday. Four years later when he was twenty-two years old, he had taken his physical and written examinations for the military. He failed the written exam and was classified 1-Y, which meant his obligation to serve in the military would be delayed.

A year later he took the test again, and again he failed. People were angry. They thought he was failing on purpose, in order to avoid going to Vietnam. How could someone who was so quick with words, they argued, fail to qualify for the Army? Here he was, they said, writing his own poetry, making a million dollars a year, and driving a brand-new red Cadillac. Yet he wasn't smart enough to carry a gun and fight for his

47

country? The angry parents of young men who had already been drafted wrote letters to their congressmen and protested.

In 1960, when Ali first registered for the draft, most Americans had never heard of Vietnam. At that time there were approximately seven hundred military advisors stationed there.

By 1965, there were 185,000 American soldiers in Vietnam, and many Americans began to feel strongly about the war. They believed it was an individual's patriotic duty to serve in the military if he was drafted. To refuse, or try to escape military service, was considered shameful by many people.

By the end of 1966 there were 400,000 American men and women stationed in Vietnam. That year the military lowered its test standards in order to draft more men. Thousands who had originally failed their written tests were now declared eligible for service. Muhammad Ali was one of them.

Ali was angry. He felt the government wanted to make an example of him because so many people were angry that he hadn't been drafted. He met with TV and newspaper reporters who were eager to hear what the Heavyweight Champion of the World had to say.

**Cassius Clay hits Russian boxer Shatkov in the 1960 Olympic boxing tournament.**

**Cassius Clay, Olympic gold medal winner, is welcomed home by his parents, and brother Rudy.**

**A triumphant Cassius Clay, wearing his Olympic gold medal, raises his hand in victory during a visit to Central High School in Louisville with his brother, Rudy (right).**

**Cassius Clay in training at Archie Moore's famous "Salt Mine" training camp.**

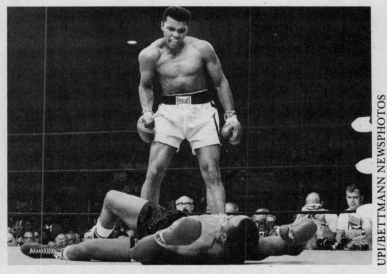

**Cassius Clay shouts at his opponent, Sonny Liston, to get up. Cassius won the 1965 fight.**

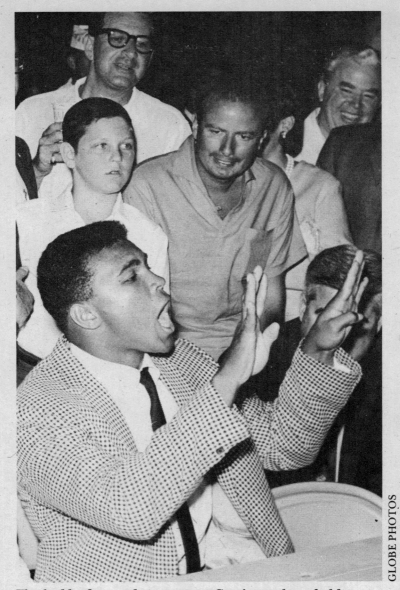

**Flanked by fans and supporters, Cassius makes a bold fight prediction.**

**Muhammad Ali waves to fans on arrival at the Army Induction Center where he refused to join the army.**

**In typical fashion, Ali "spars" with Joe Frazier over who is the *real* Heavyweight Champion.**

Ali throws a right to the head of George Foreman during the "Rumble in the Jungle."

Surrounded by his numerous awards and trophies, Ali models his World Championship belt.

**Ali successfully defends his title against Joe Frazier in the "Thrilla in Manila."**

**Muhammad Ali.**

A reporter told Ali that he would be asked to enroll in the military very soon. He replied: "Why are they gunning for me? I ain't got no quarrel with them Viet Cong."

The Viet Cong were America's opponents in the war. They were the enemy of the United States; and by saying that he had no "quarrel" with them, Ali had implied that the Viet Cong were not his enemy.

Ali's statement made headline news the next day. Many people thought it was anti-American. Muhammad Ali's position was considered radical and extreme. The Illinois Athletic Commission didn't like it. It canceled a fight Ali was supposed to have in Chicago when he would not apologize for what he had said.

On April 1, 1967, Muhammad Ali received his notice to report to the induction center at the U.S. Customs House in Houston on April 28 to enroll for military service. Within hours the whole country had heard. It was front-page news: *Army Tells Clay—Put Up or Shut Up*.

On the morning of April 28, Ali prepared himself. The night before, he ate the same dinner he did before a big fight: steak, salad, and a baked potato. His mother called. "Gee-Gee," she said, "do the right thing. If I were you, I would go ahead . . . and join the army. . . ." Ali understood his mother. It had taken her some time to accept the decision he had made about his religion. Now it would take her a while to accept his decision about the Army. "Bird, I love you. Whatever I do, Bird, remember I love you," Ali said to his mother.

On the way to the induction center he was surrounded by admirers. He signed autographs, sometimes writing "Peace" below his name.

A Navy officer escorted Ali into a large room, where he joined thirty other draftees. First they had their physical examination. Next the inductees ate lunch together. Then they were told to march down the hall to a smaller room. They all lined up. The room was quiet.

The group was ordered to stand at attention. An officer explained that when their names were called, they should take a step forward, signifying that they were willing to enter the military. He began calling out the names.

Ali's former name, "Cassius Clay," was called.

The room was silent. Ali did not move. The officer stood in front of Ali and stared at him. He called his name again. This time he said: "Cassius Clay, will you please step forward and be inducted into the armed forces of the United States?"

Ali did not move. Another officer came into the room and escorted Ali to a nearby office. There the officer explained to him that he might be charged with a crime and face five years in jail and a $10,000 fine if he refused to be inducted. The officer asked Ali if he would like to change his mind, and Ali said he would not. He signed a statement about his reasons for refusing service in the military and then left.

As he came out of the induction center, the military police had a difficult time controlling the crowds and TV cameras. The reporters shouted at Ali, asking what he had done.

He handed out a prepared statement with two reasons why he refused to be inducted. First, he was a practicing minister for the church of the Nation of Islam and ministers could not be drafted. And second, it was against his personal religious beliefs to kill someone in war.

One reporter asked him if he was willing to take the consequences of his actions. Ali told him: "Every day they die in Vietnam for nothing. I might as well die here for something."

Many people were angry with Ali's refusal to go to war. The chairman of the New York State Boxing Commission said that Ali's beliefs were "detrimental to the best interests of boxing." The commission took away his license to box in

New York State. Other states quickly followed, and in no time Ali was unable to get a license to box.

Muhammad Ali was charged with refusing to serve in the armed forces of the United States. He pleaded not guilty. When Ali's case reached the federal court, his lawyers explained that their client's beliefs were sincere. They told the story of how Ali's first fight with Sonny Liston was almost canceled just because people didn't like it that Ali was a Black Muslim. But when Ali told the promoters of the fight that he would rather give up his chance at the championship than give up his religion, the promoters went through with the fight.

The lawyers told the court about the millions of dollars Ali had passed up by refusing to do commercials and refusing the movie roles that were offered to him. Ali did so because his religion said that these activities were not in the best interests of his fellow black Americans.

Ali's lawyers gave four reasons why Ali was asking to be excused from military service: his religion did not allow him to fight in a war not approved by Allah; he was a practicing minister and ministers were not drafted; there was not a fair representation of blacks on the draft boards;

and, as a black man, he could not fight against the dark-skinned people of Vietnam.

In June Ali was found guilty of draft evasion. He was fined 10,000 dollars and given the maximum sentence: five years in prison. But he did not go to jail because his lawyers were appealing the case. This meant that they would take it to a more powerful court.

Although he did not go to jail, Ali was still unable to fight in the United States since most states had taken away his license to fight. Ali tried to fight abroad, but the government wouldn't let him. They canceled his passport. Ali assumed that the government was worried that he wouldn't come back and face his punishment. To assure them that he would, he offered to give the government 100,000 dollars to keep until he came back. He also offered to give the government 70 percent of the money he made until he returned. But the government still wouldn't allow him to leave the United States to fight in another country.

Ali couldn't get a license to fight in the country, and now he wasn't allowed to leave to fight outside the country. The Heavyweight Champion could no longer earn his living by boxing.

# The Comeback

When Ali's lawyers appealed his conviction, they told the court that he was going to run out of money if he wasn't allowed to earn a living. Boxing was the only profession that he had. Although he had made millions, he had also spent millions. His taxes were high, and the fees of his lawyers were getting bigger every day. If he had to appeal his case all the way to the Supreme Court, that would cost a lot of money.

Ali had to pay $15,000 a year in alimony to his first wife. And now he had a new wife and family to support. Ali's new wife was Belinda Boyds, whom he married in 1967. They had been introduced by Herbert Muhammad. She had been a Black Muslim all her life. The year after they were married, they had a child. The year after that, they had twins.

Now that he wasn't boxing, for the first time in almost fifteen years Muhammad Ali did not have to train every day. He tried to use the free time as best he could. He enjoyed being with his family, and he began to educate himself about the world around him. He often traveled around the country and spoke at various Muslim temples. He also lectured at college campuses, where he was very popular.

Speaking at Muslim temples and on college campuses was a challenge. Bragging before a boxing match was one thing, but speaking in an auditorium full of people was another. Ali learned to become a good speaker by using the same work habits that made him a great boxer. He practiced in front of a mirror, and his wife acted as a critic. He practiced until he got it right.

He worked at all sorts of things he had never thought of doing when he was boxing full-time. He worked as a commentator for ABC-TV during a USA/USSR boxing tournament. And he wrote his autobiography, *The Greatest*, with the help of Richard Durham. He even acted in a Broadway play.

Ali did his best to stay in shape. He ran and sparred occasionally, but his heart wasn't in it. As the weeks turned into months, he wondered whether he would ever fight again.

As the months turned into years, Ali's appeal worked its way through the courts. During that time, many Americans were changing their opinions about the war in Vietnam. People were becoming deeply concerned as more soldiers were sent there to fight.

Muhammad Ali's stand was not as unpopular as it once was. A growing number of Americans wanted to hear what he had to say. In addition to lecturing at colleges across the country, he spoke at political rallies. A poll showed that he was one of the most popular speakers in the country.

Publicly, Ali said he did not care about ever boxing again. In truth, he couldn't wait to get back in the ring. He wanted to regain the title he believed was his.

In June 1971, after four years of costly legal battles, the Supreme Court agreed to hear the case of the *United States v. Muhammad Ali*. In an 8–0 decision, the court said that he was sincere in his religious beliefs and should not be punished in any way. Ali had won what he called "the biggest victory of my life."

During the time Ali couldn't fight, the question of who was the *real* Heavyweight Champ became confusing. The World Boxing Association (WBA) held an eight-man elimination tournament and in the spring of 1968, Jimmy Ellis defeated Jerry Quarry to become the WBA champion. But most fight fans considered Joe Frazier the champ. Frazier had refused to participate in the WBA tournament. He felt he was a better fighter than anyone in the tournament, and most people agreed. He didn't think he had to enter a tournament and fight his way to the top when he was already there. "I'm going to let them fight it out. And if Clay comes back, I'll be waiting for him," Frazier said.

In February 1970, Frazier defeated Jimmy Ellis, winning the championship and clearing up most of the confusion. But many fight fans agreed that Ali was the *real* champ. Once he started to fight again, however, he would have to prove himself by fighting all of the contenders.

Muhammad Ali had begun his comeback a year before the Supreme Court ruling. Herbert Muhammad had never stopped trying to get him a license to box, and finally his efforts paid off. Ali was allowed to fight Jerry Quarry in Atlanta on October 26, 1970. Even though Quarry had lost to Ellis, he was still a top contender. The fight was great news for Ali. Now that Georgia had granted him a license, maybe other states would, too.

Ali had only six weeks to train. That was not a lot of time, considering he hadn't boxed in three years. He went to Miami Beach, Florida, to train.

This fight would be more than just another fight. Some people did not want a black man to be the champ. They wanted Jerry Quarry, who was white, to win. Others thought Ali's championship title had been unfairly taken away from him. They wanted him to win it back. In the years since he had started boxing, Ali had become the hero of many black Americans, and many boxing fans, black and white, wanted him to win.

Downtown Atlanta was turned into one big party for the fight. People from all over the country came to celebrate the "return of the king."

Many famous black Americans were there. Diana Ross, Bill Cosby, Sidney Poitier, and Hank Aaron led a long list of actors, entertainers, and athletes. Jesse Jackson and Mrs. Martin Luther King, Jr. came along with other important political leaders.

The night of the fight, Atlanta looked more like Hollywood. The chauffeur-driven cars rolled up to the hotel entrances one after another. The people who stepped out of the cars were all elaborately dressed. There were parties everywhere.

At the press conferences before the fight, Ali was unusually quiet. There were no poems or predictions, and there was no bragging. He still had his sense of humor, but he was more cautious. He stayed away from any political discussions.

The weigh-in was not as quiet. But it wasn't Ali who was the center of attention this time. Jerry Quarry didn't like the two doctors who had been assigned to the fight. They were black, and Quarry was worried that they would favor Ali because he was black, too.

Ali watched the scene Jerry caused at the weigh-in. He thought about all the fights he had fought when the doctors were white.

Ali and Quarry were asked to pose for the cameras. The photographer requested that they put their heads together so he could get them both in the shot. Ali whispered in Jerry's ear: "I'm gonna whip you till you're cherry red. You insulted all those black doctors."

Ali had changed—but not completely.

\*     \*     \*

When the fighters were introduced to the crowd, Ali came out of his corner, arms held high. He did the "Ali shuffle"—criss-crossing his legs with amazing speed. The standing-room-only audience erupted with wild cheering.

In the first round Ali attacked Jerry immediately. He landed a number of punches and combinations to the face. In the second round Ali looked a little slower. But his lightning-quick combinations were still hurting Jerry. In the third round the fight had to be stopped. There was a bad cut over Jerry's eye. Ali won on a technical knockout.

After the fight, Mrs. Martin Luther King, Jr. called Ali a "champion of justice, peace, and unity." Ali was given the Martin Luther King award.

By beating Jerry Quarry, Ali not only came closer to regaining his championship title, he also became an important role model in the black community. But Jerry Quarry was just the first step on Ali's long road back to becoming the Heavyweight Champion of the World. Before Ali could challenge Joe Frazier, he had to fight Oscar Bonavena, a big heavyweight fighter from Argentina. He and Ali were scheduled to fight in New York City on December 7, 1970.

Ali did not take Bonavena seriously. He did

not train as he had for the Quarry fight. On the day of the fight Ali enjoyed himself, walking the streets of New York. He stopped on street corners and in department stores. He gave short speeches and signed autographs. He got back to the hotel only a few hours before the fight. Then, at the last minute, Ali decided not to take the limousine to the fight but to ride the subway instead. Subway riders could hardly believe their eyes when they saw Muhammad Ali on the way to his fight!

Ali came out for the first round looking heavy and dull. His punches didn't have the speed and accuracy that everyone had come to expect. But Bonavena was still no match for him. In the last round Ali knocked Bonavena out.

With Jerry Quarry and Oscar Bonavena out of the way, Muhammad Ali was ready to meet Joe Frazier—now the undisputed Heavyweight Champion.

# Collision Course

Joe Frazier's nickname was "Smokin' Joe," and it fit. His left hook was dangerous enough to flatten any foe. And nothing seemed to make Joe Frazier tired.

Frazier was considered a good person and a hardworking fighter. Still he was not very popular, and he blamed that on Muhammad Ali. He felt he did not get the respect he deserved because he spent his whole career fighting in Ali's shadow. Defeating Ali, he thought, would earn him that respect.

During the time that Ali could not fight because of his stand on the Vietnam War, Frazier waited. He knew Ali would return to fighting, and Frazier would challenge him. But that didn't make Ali nervous. "Joe Frazier is just another contender now that I have a license," he said.

The Ali and Frazier fight had the same kind of tension that surrounded the fights just after Muhammad Ali had changed his name from Cassius Clay. Frazier refused to call Ali anything but Cassius Clay, and he said that Clay was a phony.

The fight was set for March 8, 1971, in New York's Madison Square Garden. They were each to receive 2.5 million dollars—win, lose, or draw. It was the largest amount of money ever paid to an athlete.

Twenty-three million people were expected to see the fight on closed-circuit TV. Fight fans called it "The Fight of the Century." It matched the powerful slugger, Joe Frazier, against the boxing master, Muhammad Ali. It matched a fighter who constantly moved forward with a fighter who danced from side to side, a man with a deadly left hook against one with blazing fast combinations. It was power versus speed.

Frazier trained in upstate New York, away from everyone. He ran six miles a day over rocky hills and boxed eight to ten rounds. He trained harder than he ever had before.

Ali trained in Miami Beach. Each day there

were crowds to watch him go through his routine. Although he took Frazier seriously, Ali didn't push himself to the limit.

Frazier spent the hours before the fight in his hotel suite. He played his guitar and relaxed with friends. Ali was surrounded by people in his suite. For over three hours he talked about everything that came into his head. From time to time he got up and shadowboxed as he talked. Of course he had prepared a poem especially for this fight:

Joe's gonna come smokin'
And I ain't gonna be jokin'
I'll be peckin' and a pokin'
Pouring water on his smokin'
This may shock and amaze ya'
But I'm gonna retire Joe Frazier.

Both fighters entered the ring dressed to dazzle. Frazier wore jade and gold trunks. The names of his five children were embroidered on the back of his $300 robe. Ali wore red velvet trunks and white shoes with red tassels on them. They bounced as he moved.

In the first few rounds Ali looked like the young Ali. He hit Frazier with a lot of punches, but Frazier kept fighting.

In the third round Frazier pushed Ali up against the ropes and hit him. Ali looked out at the audience and shook his head "No." He wanted the crowd to know that Frazier couldn't hurt him. Applause and laughter broke out around ringside.

By the middle of the fight it was about even. Ali had won the opening rounds, but Frazier was winning the later ones.

In the eighth, ninth, and tenth rounds, Ali looked as though he was losing strength. In the eleventh, Frazier hit him with a solid punch to the head. Ali's legs buckled, and his eyes looked glassy. He was hurt, and the crowd was stunned.

The fight was close. In the fourteenth round Ali came on strong, hoping that Frazier was tired. Then, in the fifteenth, Frazier hit Ali with a rock-hard left hook. Ali's eyes closed and his legs folded under him. He went down and instinctively rolled onto one elbow. Ali was down, but he was not out. By the count of three he was up. His jaw was already swollen from the blow. And his entire body throbbed with pain.

Then he heard the ring announcer: "The winner, by unanimous decision, the undisputed World Heavyweight Champion Joe Frazier." Joe Frazier had successfully defended his title. People poured into the ring, pushing their way past the police. Frazier's face was swollen almost beyond recognition. He went over to Ali's corner and told him he had fought a great fight. Ali told Frazier he was now the champ. Frazier was carried to his dressing room. Later he was taken to a hospital for six weeks to recover.

Ali was glad it was over. He wanted to go home and see his wife and children. Only a few people were allowed in Ali's dressing room, and one was his mother. She told her son he "did a fine job for someone who's been out of the ring for so long . . .you fought a good fight."

This was Ali's first loss as a professional boxer, and it came close to destroying his confidence and ending his career. He knew he would have to work hard for a rematch with Frazier. He took a long hard look inside himself. He said, "When you win so long, so much, you forget. You think your name will win. You forget the sacrifices, the work that goes into winning. Now I'm down. They say I'm finished. They're celebrating. But I'll come back."

# "Rumble in the Jungle"

Muhammad Ali had paid a high price for his religious beliefs. Financially he had lost millions because he was unable to fight. Physically the toll might have been even greater. Many people felt that he had fought his best against Frazier—but that his best just wasn't good enough.

Ali wanted that rematch with Frazier. He knew that if he didn't beat Joe Frazier, he would never be considered the champion.

Three months after losing to Frazier he began to prepare for a rematch. In July he took on his old sparring partner, Jimmy Ellis, and knocked him out in the twelfth round. He fought two more times in 1971, and he won both fights. In 1972 he fought and won six times, four by knockouts. He fought all over the world—in

Zurich, Switzerland; Tokyo, Japan; Vancouver, Canada; Dublin, Ireland; and Djakarta, Indonesia.

In March 1973, Ali fought Ken Norton, another step on his road back to the championship. Ali didn't think Norton had a chance. He didn't bother to train hard for the fight. The night before, he was up till the morning hours entertaining people in the hotel coffee shop.

Ali came into the ring wearing a robe given to him by Elvis Presley. It said *The People's Champ* on the back. Ali weighed 221 pounds and looked flabby around the middle.

From the moment of the opening bell, Ali seemed sluggish. His punches had little power to them. In the second round Norton sent a crashing left to Ali's jaw. He felt a sharp pain and could taste blood in his throat. When he went to his corner between rounds, he asked how he could tell if his jaw was broken. He was told it would make a sound like two plates struck together. Ali tried it and could hear the sound. He refused to stop fighting, however, even though there were more than thirteen rounds to go. He felt he could still win. But it turned out that he couldn't.

Ken Norton was awarded a split decision. Joe Frazier jumped into the ring to hug Norton, his former sparring partner. By now, the pain in Ali's face was almost more than he could stand. He waved to his wife before he was whisked out of sight. That night he was sent to the hospital to have his jaw set.

After the Norton fight many of Ali's fans abandoned him. Howard Cosell predicted that he was finished. The three and a half years that he hadn't fought had simply been too much, people said. The newspaper headlines the next day told the whole story: *Muhammad Is Finished; End of an Era; Beaten by a Nobody; Big Mouth Shut for All Time.*

Ali headed for Louisville with his wife and Maryum, their daughter. He needed to rest and to see the people who cared about him. He went to Aunt Coretta's for a family reunion. He spent long hours with Bird and Cash. He rested.

Six months later Muhammad Ali was ready for his return bout with Norton. This time he trained hard for the fight, and he shed nine pounds.

It was a close fight all the way. Norton was the more aggressive fighter as Ali danced away from danger. This time, Ali won the split decision. But there were many who felt that Norton had won the fight.

Ali had to fight George Foreman now. Foreman first came to attention in the 1968 Olympics when he won the gold medal for heavyweight boxing. He was nineteen years old then.

Since turning pro, Foreman had won his first thirty-eight fights, thirty-five by knockouts. He had the highest knockout percentage in the history of boxing. In January 1973, when he was twenty-four years old, Foreman took the championship away from Joe Frazier when he destroyed him in a match that lasted only four minutes and twenty-five seconds. At 6'3", 215 pounds, Foreman was now the most powerful opponent Muhammad Ali had ever faced.

Ali trained in secret for four months in a camp he had bought in the Pocono Mountains of Pennsylvania. He ate a healthful diet of fresh vegetables, veal and fish, distilled water and fruit juices. He knew that the way to win was to train harder than the actual match would be. That way the match would seem easier, and he would have the strength to win.

Ali invented a strategy for the fight. He called it "rope-a-dope." Ali knew he was not as fast as he used to be. So his plan was to tire Foreman out. He planned to lie on the ropes and let Foreman hit him. The ropes would help absorb the power of Foreman's punches. In that way he could take the punches, but they would not do much damage. The punching, he thought, would tire Foreman out.

The odds were four to one against Ali. The sports headlines in the *Chicago Tribune* read *Ali Needs a Miracle*. People thought that Ali was too old, that he didn't stand a chance.

On October 30, 1974, the fight was all set to go. Ali called it the "Rumble in the Jungle" because they were fighting in an African country called Zaire. Ali believed that it was important to fight in places like Zaire so that the white world could become more familiar with the non-white world.

Ali came into the open-air stadium filled with 63,000 fans. He was escorted by twenty men.

At the center of the ring, the referee gave the two fighters their last-minute instructions. Ali said to Foreman, "You have heard of me since you were young. You've been following me since you were a little boy. Now you must meet me, your master."

Ali did everything he had trained to do. His strategy worked. Foreman was confused from the opening bell. Ali hit him with rights, rather than lefts, going against all the rules. He caught Foreman off guard. The frustration was visible on Foreman's face. By the sixth round Foreman had run out of steam. In the eighth, Ali hit

Foreman with a brilliant combination of punches, and Foreman fell forward. When he left the ring, he was still dazed.

Ali had fooled the experts again. At thirty-two years old he had recaptured the title of Heavyweight Champion of the World against tremendous odds!

# "Thrilla in Manila"

Just five months after the "Rumble in the Jungle" Ali began fighting to defend his title. He fought four times in 1975 and won every fight. But fans would remember only the fight against Joe Frazier that took place on September 30 in the Asian country of the Philippines. This fight came to be known as the "Thrilla in Manila."

Ali had won his rematch with Frazier in January 1974. Now he was fighting Frazier again— to defend his championship title.

When he arrived in Manila, the capital of the Philippines, Ali was treated like royalty. He was received by President Marcos and his wife and followed by crowds wherever he went. Frazier arrived in the country quietly and was largely ignored.

While Ali enjoyed his celebrity status, Frazier passed the time quietly in his hotel suite playing cards with his sparring partners.

The government had invested $4 million to have the fight in their country. Frazier would earn $2 million and Ali was expected to get over $4.5 million. An estimated 700 million people would be watching on closed-circuit TV in sixty-four countries.

Everyone expected this fight to be tremendous. Joe Frazier and Muhammad Ali were the two best fighters in modern boxing history. This fight would settle, once and for all, who was the best.

The fans were not disappointed. Both men fought their hearts out. Every round was a battle, without a moment's rest. This fight was about the will to win.

The first few rounds went to Ali, who came out blazing. Ali hit Frazier with his familiar assortment of clean, stinging shots to the head. They were doing damage, but they weren't slowing Frazier down.

By the fourth round Frazier was getting stronger. He was gaining confidence. Frazier began to dominate the fight. Ali was moving but not as he had in the early rounds. He was not landing as many punches, and Frazier kept coming. His powerful punches were crashing through Ali's upraised hands.

Ali continued to rely on his movements and combinations. But Frazier, bobbing up and down at the waist, ducked under most of them. It was clear that neither fighter was going to be knocked out. The stamina and strength of the two men were remarkable. Someone would have to give up for the fight to end.

In the tenth round, Frazier hit Ali with a powerful shot that buckled Ali's legs. To many it was miraculous that Ali didn't go down right then and there.

It looked as though Ali were losing as the twelfth round ended. Then, in the thirteenth, Ali did what he had done so many times before. He found the strength to make a final, valiant effort.

Ali hit Frazier with as much strength as he had in the opening rounds. By now Frazier had taken a lot of punishment. His face was bloodied, and his eyes were almost swollen shut. Ali circled Frazier; snap, snap, snapping his gloves past Frazier's tired arms and into his face.

Amazingly, Ali came out even stronger in the fourteenth round. He hit Frazier so hard that the exhausted fighter's mouthpiece flew into the seats below. Ali hit Frazier at will throughout the round. Frazier had no strength left in his arms or legs. He could no longer see—he could only stand there and take it. But he wouldn't go down. Mercifully, the bell rang to end the fourteenth.

When the fifteenth and final round began, Ali was up, but where was Frazier? Frazier was not coming out.

Eddie Futch, Frazier's trainer, knew that his fighter had taken enough punches. Just one more round could be one round too many. Frazier was dazed and couldn't see out of either eye. Futch put his hand on Frazier's shoulder and told him the fight was over.

Frazier pleaded with Futch to let him go, but he wasn't going anywhere. The "Thrilla in Manila" was over. Ali won! It was a technical knockout.

When Ali realized what had happened, he lay down right there on the canvas. All he could think was, "It's over." It was the hardest fight he had ever fought.

Afterwards, Ali had two things to say: "Frazier's the greatest fighter of all time . . . next to me. . . . What you saw was next to death."

# The Last Round

**M**any people believe that Muhammad Ali should have retired after the "Thrilla in Manila." But Ali didn't retire, perhaps because he needed the money. Some people thought he didn't retire because he wasn't ready to admit that anyone could beat him.

On February 15, 1978, thirty-six-year-old Muhammad Ali met twenty-four-year-old Leon Spinks. Spinks was the light-heavyweight gold medal winner from the 1976 Olympics. He had fought only seven professional fights and had never fought more than ten rounds. The experts said Spinks was clearly the underdog.

Spinks was twelve years younger than Ali. But Ali was confident that his conditioning and determination would once again carry the day. He planned to tire out his young opponent.

Ali gave away the early rounds to Spinks. He connected with some solid punches in the tenth, but it was not enough. Spinks upset Ali and became the new Heavyweight Champion of the World. Ali accepted his defeat gracefully. He said that he lost "simply because Spinks was better."

Six months later Ali had a return match with Spinks. He fought with all the wisdom he had gained from twenty years in the ring. He easily outpointed Spinks and won a fifteen-round decision. Muhammad Ali was now the first man in history to win the heavyweight championship three times. Friends and associates begged him to retire. He agreed, but not for long.

In late 1980, when he was thirty-eight, Ali came out of a two-year retirement to fight the current champion, Larry Holmes. He would earn $8 million for the fight. Holmes was Ali's former sparring partner. He had gone to Zaire with him to train for the Foreman fight. Since becoming champion in 1978, when Ali was in retirement, Holmes had defended his title seven times, winning each time by a knockout. After thirty-five fights he was unbeaten.

Once again Ali went to the Poconos to train.

He trained the hardest he had ever trained. When he started out, he weighed 254 pounds, but he soon brought it down to 212. This was the lightest he'd been since he had fought Foreman.

But the fight was simply no contest. Ali's punches had no sting. He moved slowly. His timing was off, and his reflexes were gone. Holmes pounded Ali for ten consecutive rounds. Ali was unable to come out for the eleventh. It was the first time in fifty-nine bouts that he could not finish a fight.

A year later Ali fought Trevor Berbick and lost. He was one month away from forty. This fight really was his last.

Now Ali had other responsibilities to think about. His career earnings when he retired were estimated at $55 million. His finances, however, were in some trouble. He was now divorced for the second time and was paying alimony and child support to two former wives. Although he had made a lot of money, he had spent a lot, and given away a lot, too, to the Nation of Islam and to friends who needed it. Since his retirement, he had made one bad business deal after another.

Ali announced business ventures that either never happened or didn't succeed. In the Fall of 1986 he announced that Ali Motors was going to sell the ALI 3WC (Ali 3-Time World Champion). Color choices were Olympic Gold, Glove Red, Knockout Black. But not one car ever rolled off the assembly line.

Another idea that didn't work was a training camp for young boxers called Champion Sports Management. A training camp was an ideal way for Ali to invest his money and use his experience, but it never happened.

In September 1984, Muhammad Ali checked into New York City's Columbia Presbyterian Medical Center. For two years journalists and people around Ali had been worried. They noticed he was having problems with his hand-eye coordination. Herbert Muhammad and Angelo Dundee had been worried about Ali's slurred speech for a while. Sometimes it was hard to understand what he was saying.

In the summer of 1984 when Ali appeared at the Los Angeles Olympics, he did not recognize friends, and he didn't even smile as fans cheered him.

Doctors discovered that Ali had been suffering since 1981 from Parkinson's syndrome. Parkinson's syndrome is a disease of the brain that slurs speech and slows movement. Coordination can be affected, and fatigue can come and go without warning. The doctors felt that Ali's condition had been caused by the blows to his head that he had received in boxing. Although he had been untouched throughout most of his career, the Frazier, Norton, Foreman, and Holmes fights had been brutal.

Many people traced Ali's problems back to his refusal to be inducted into the Army. The three and a half years of inactivity, they said, had caused him to change his lifestyle. When he returned to boxing, his legs could no longer move as speedily and as tirelessly as they once did. He could no longer afford to keep his distance. To win he had to move closer to his opponent, and so he took more punches.

At a press conference at the hospital, Ali said: "I've been in the boxing ring for thirty years, and I've taken a lot of punches. So there is a great possibility that something could be wrong. . . . I am not suffering, I just feel tired. . . ."

Then he paused and said: "I'll whip this thing."

Today Muhammad Ali is still fighting Parkinson's syndrome. He is now married to Yolanda Williams. He and "Lonnie" grew up across the street from each other in Louisville. They live on an eighty-eight-acre farm in Berrien Springs, Michigan.

Ali tries to stay in shape by taking long walks, riding a bicycle, and shadowboxing.

Although there is a slight slurring of his speech and sometimes he doesn't walk so well, he has no pain. When he gets tired in the afternoon, he takes a nap.

He spends a good deal of his time working on behalf of his religion. He wants to correct what he believes is misunderstanding of the teachings of the Nation of Islam. He distributes a book that helps explain Islam, and he is writing his own religious pamphlet.

In 1988, reflecting on his career and his illness, Ali said: "If you told me I could go back in my life and start over healthy and that with boxing this would happen—stay Cassius Clay and it wouldn't—I'd take this route. It was worth it."

# Boxing Vocabulary

**Combination:** a number of quick punches using both hands.

**Counterpunch:** a punch thrown in response to your opponent's first punch.

**(A Right) Cross:** a punch thrown when your opponent throws a left. Your right crosses over his left.

**Decision:** the official verdict at the end of a fight where there is no knockout. The outcome used to be decided by the votes of a referee and two judges. Now, in most cases, the referee does not vote, and the decision is made by three judges.

*Split Decision:* two of the three judges agree on a winner.

*Unanimous Decision:* all three judges agree on a winner.

**Fixed:** when the outcome of a fight is decided in advance. It usually occurs when the fighter favored to win allows himself to be knocked out. The fighter is paid to do this by people who are going to bet on the fight and make a lot of money. Fixed fights can also involve judges and referees.

**Grudge Match:** a fight between two boxers who have developed a genuine dislike for each other.

**Handlers:** a boxer's trainer, assistant trainer, and whoever else is in his corner during a fight.

**Hook:** a short, swinging punch thrown with the arm rigid but the elbow bent. It is usually used at close range.

**Jab:** a short, quick, straight punch, usually thrown with the left hand. It is used to keep your opponent off balance, rather than knock him out. It is often used to set up other punches or combinations.

**Knockout:** when an opponent is beaten because he has been hit so hard he remains on the floor for ten seconds.

**Mouthpiece:** a rubber or plastic device that is clenched between the upper and lower teeth. It can prevent injury to the teeth, mouth, and jaw.

**One-Two Punch:** two punches, thrown quickly, one right after the other. The left is usually thrown first.

**Shadowboxing:** boxing against an imaginary opponent to improve skills.

**Spar:** to box for exercise, amusement, or training.

**Speed Bag:** a small punching bag that is used to develop timing and hand-eye coordination.

**Technical Knockout:** when the referee stops a fight because a fighter is injured, unable to protect himself, or quits.

**Weigh-in:** recording the weight of the two fighters on official scales. It is usually done the day before the fight, or the day of a fight, often at noon.